Burn it All Down,
Then Kiss Me

Dearest gentle reader,

I hope you find something
new, inspirational or disruptive
in these!

Love,

Kate MacAlister

Gate x

for the comrades, the lovers and the witches

"Let's go,
and you, my star, next to me,
newborn from my own clay,
you will have found the hidden spring
and in the midst of the fire, you will be
next to me,
with your wild eyes,
raising my flag."

-   *The Flag, Pablo Neruda*

Praise for Burn it All Down, Then Kiss Me

"Come toss those old bones into the fire... *Burn it All Down, Then Kiss Me* invites readers to embrace a self-destructive love that will inevitably end in flames, weaving a poetic journey of passion and pain. With gothic femininity and modern sensibilities, Kate MacAlister's collection explores the delicate balance between the fire of passion and the soothing sea of peace. These poems ignite a sinewy visceral rage while guiding us to find our own remedies for life's pain. A mesmerizing blend of natural imagery and enchanting rituals, it evokes a sense of sacrifice and the pursuit of lasting love. MacAlister's words are a poetic inferno that ignites the imagination and leaves us yearning for more." — Kate Gough, author of *The Maiden in the Tower*

"MacAlister invites readers on a journey of resilience and liberation with poetry that takes you by the hand and leads you through pages of rebellion, justice, and ultimately, love. Dispelling myths, challenging societal norms with a unique softness. Her words, bound by passion, become synonymous with hope." — Faye Alexandra Rose, author of *Pneuma*

"Kate MacAlister's second collection, *Burn it All Down, Then Kiss Me*, weaves a spellbinding tapestry of ritual magic and transformative flames. With the melodic cadence of an arcane spell, McAllister breaks free from traditional forms, captivating readers with her mesmerizing freeform poetry. Themes of body, earth, and mystic powers intertwine, coaxing a simmering fury to the surface. In this collection, MacAlister's words ignite like an enraged bonfire, fueling the fiery inner strength of femininity. MacAlister's poetry is a wake-up call that will leave readers burning with passion and dreaming of revolution."
— Sarah Herrin, *EIC of Beyond the Veil Press*

In the opening pages of this book, Kate MacAlister welcomes us to a state of sleeping. We are enlightened to an energy long idle in a state of dormancy and it is waking up. Poems 'r i t u a l' and 'summoning' create an anticipation for the flames about to ignite. MacAlister gathers momentum with 'tfw… you burn the patriarchy to the ground,' alluding to the unity of sisterhood, bringing the reader to the centre of a coven ready to take their stakes. *Burn it All Down, Then Kiss Me* is a violently beautiful collection about sisterhood, opposition and taking a stand. It is an unforgettable book from a poet who never fails to persist against the constraints of what is expected. — Chloe Hanks, author of *I Call Upon the Witches*

"Burn It All Down, Then Kiss Me" is a bitingly honest reflection of the world around us, flames, blood, love, and all. The collection breathes new life into a modern revolution with the radical hindsight of the ones who came before her. With a fearless and loving determination to burn commonplace oppression to the ground, MacAlister takes readers to "the edge of the world", only to remind us how much of it we have left, if only we join the fight."
— A. Griffin, author of *even God didn't want grief*

In poetry that serves as a call to change the status quo, or a push for change, it is easy to fall into a trap of blind anger that ends up repetitive and degrading, rather than uplifting. MacAlister, however, navigates these waters with grace, perfectly balancing both fury and hope to encourage her readers to dream of a better world, rather than simply tearing one down. In Burn it All Down, Then Kiss Me, readers will never feel disconnected or disengaged. MacAlister has mastered the art of creating stories through her poetry. As a writer, she has exhibited impressive uses of imagery, a wide variety of styles, and a broad range of emotion - but that isn't what makes this collection special. It is the core humanity of it, the connections MacAlister draws between herself and her audience and the world as a whole, that makes this book one of the most spectacular collections I have read. — *Gitika Sanjay*

Contents

Foreword

Kate MacAlister's poetry collection, Burn it All Down, Then Kiss Me, is a fierce and unapologetic call to arms, an urgent reminder of the power of words to inspire, provoke, and ultimately, transform. Each poem in this collection is a weapon against complacency, a rallying cry for justice, and a testament to the resilience of the human spirit.

The title poem encapsulates the spirit of the collection perfectly. It is a bold and fiery declaration of rebellion, a passionate plea to tear down the structures that oppress us and build something new in their place. But it is also a tender and intimate expression of love, a recognition of the beauty that can arise from destruction and the hope that can emerge from the ashes.

Throughout the collection, MacAlister tackles themes of identity, politics, love, and loss with unflinching honesty and unwavering courage. "Hypnagogia" and "Take Care of Each Other to Be Dangerous Together" are both visceral and evocative, capturing the essence of the human experience and the emotions that come with it.

This collection is a testament to the power of language and the resilience of the human spirit. It's a call to arms, a call to love, and a call to action. MacAlister's poetry is not for the faint of heart. It is a battle cry, a challenge to confront the darkness within and without. Burn it All Down is a powerful and timely collection that demands to be read, shared, and embraced.

Rebecca Rijsdijk, Editor-in-Chief Sunday Mornings at the River, April 2023

r i t u a l

light the evening fire
I stir within my sister's
dream forest
lead me

I must become
I have been and
I must become
more

the ground waits for
old blood, wet earth

I see her dance
at home in torn flesh
her fangs set with amber
and dew

where her teeth
have been in me
even you know that
the flesh knows
better than the spirit
what the soul has eyes for

quiet now, she turns to gold
you come apart in her hands
she falls on your farewell heart

it is why there is so much blood
in sacrifice

summoning

I.   The Allotter

incessant, bewildering moon-talk
hush, the lullaby is just a nightmare
the pedestal fine, but fading
all my sins: I lay them down for you
a clarity spread
the Lovers
the Moon
my High-priestess

II.   The Spinner

maybe waking maybe dying
cull and concoct the remedies for
a millennia of sleep paralysis
dress the wounds
their names embalmed
in twilight fragrance
the secrets of the troubadour queen
inextricably bound
cast the circle

III.   The Unturnable

the body is watered imagination
needle and thread
the thread will always be picked up again
a thread broken means Death
weave the shroud in open surrender
reclaim the words and feed them to each other
shelter in the chasm of the heart

made of earth
I charge this path to be
worthy of your sacred knees
let healing bleed from my hands and eyes
invoke the elements

call me Fury call me Rage call me Stormtide   call me

the Deep Blue

draw down the firmament
don't falter at the sight
turn to me now
your name fated you
to see in the dark

burn it all down, then kiss me

bring in the voices

we bring you

the story of mass resignations and strikes, futile calls to
o p e n
breakdowns   strategy chokepoints   a promise-free
world awaits

the stories of a cratered church, a ruin - always a glimpse of
the past as well as the future

the stories of nothing at all   think of fumes
decomposing imagination
consult the oracle, refresh the screen, the scream

steepen the questions about the fall of the rich and the
powerful

it still costs a fee to see the ruins
it costs nothing to tell the story
it costs everything to tell the story
— truly.

we bring you

        the stories of what happened here
lost to the foundations of wealth and poverty

the stories of those who paint with the colour of all people.
 grief and struggle, grey internalised.

a story of the resistance is a record failure   the first-hand
account of the cruelty of a system
sleepwalking up against the walls

the stories of raising questions   there is no greater failure
than to join the ranks of those
who hold you   down

there has always been
another way

we bring you

all power to the sparks when the sirens scream silence

shine alight in mutual aid
work on abolition
we invite you to

o p e n

come toss those old bones
into the fire

may queen

white linen sailboats
on electrical currents
are caught in
tricoloured nets of wires

the screaming
blinking
lifelines
illuminate the room
brighter than any star

every night I begin again

how many beats per minute
for a breaking heart?

and we cannot remember
and we cannot recall
to whom we sacrifice
on this overgrown
altar

vowed to stillness in
a world behind glass
all our smiles are spent
as we constantly
worship
in the deepest
Dark
-the lost hours
before the dawn

who do we pray to
when the air is on fire?

and the end of the road
is scattered carelessly with
wings and souls of
forgotten heroes?

the chill in my bones
is a feverish fear
desperately shrouded beneath
the memory of standing ovations
and this delicate mask

so I may sing gentle lullabies
to catch your
bleeding breath
that
paints
strange blue flowers
on your porcelain lips

I hold you so close
to my chest
as if all this raging love
were an inspiration
for your shattered lungs

that last kiss
will always taste of
the longest night.

melusine

cut me deeper
as we hide beneath the floorboards
creaking with your strange rebellion

it is centuries old

my hunger is a shapeshifting oath
a castle of rage and sand
a home full of silver scales
a tidal wave pouring moon songs

out of my hair
into your hands
a wishing
well
a prayer
holy from the waist
down

at sunset
the long shadows
become blackened pages
tangled in seaweed
where you and I are
sea serpents
sirens
enchantingly
calling for Death
to all men

all that is left
for the ritual is
to collect the husks
and shells

please hold
my sea glass
between the small wrecks and reefs
of your scarred porcelain fingers
don't wash me out
tomorrow

please hold
my heart in that
vast ocean of your calling
cast on the dark-legged sky

witness the rebirth of venus
in a storm of salt
in my mortal eyes

I don't care
about the broken things
we leave behind

just drive.

canticle

all the battles
of every day
burn our candle low

let me take you
deep into the forest
where light breeds in the dark

Would it be too much?
Would it be impolite?

to offer you my blood
flowers
in a porcelain vessel of moonlight
by the sleeping river

where we hungered
where we touched

Death became small
remained heavy
stars falling from your eyes
through my bones
burning my roughened edges

nothing can feed
the wilderness of mine
but the sound of your soft voice

I hear
the whispered song of
your scars in
every night
nothing can feed

Kate MacAlister

the soft fauna of mine
but the sound of your wild heart

all my scratches and stitches
utter but one prayer

please don't change your mind

maybe this is where
courage blossoms

23

the moon

whale songs run aground in the sand, unfolding the soft
shoreline of your clavicle - calling
murmurations of bones, spread like seagull wings, so bound
beneath the skin.

the gushing scent of the tide drowns out the gravity, if only
for these keepsake moments.
come up close. dive deeper and examine the violent
anatomy of wreckage with me?

a skeletal emergence, the pulse still throbbing, the coral
spine still standing overgrown with longing.
I adorn you with the black seashells of gold-rushed days,
urgently pressed against your chest.

I hear the waves beating in every chamber of your heart.
What has been locked inside?
wish three times upon this current; we are made of the
same offbeat dream.

and even if it kills me, why don't you flood me now?

you sing and I will come.
you sing... and I will come
you sing. I will come.

the sea

reanimating all forgotten places. what an awakening in a
midnight castle of sand:
ships in the night smashed on the same shore, breaking
between the push and the pull.

rise night after night in the borrowed light. taste the
demure, the unholy, the shallow
mercy of wind and beach glass, beneath a mirror infinitely
coiling, downwards, downwards.

this twilight dawn of worlds changing stains my thighs with
salt water and strange goodbyes.
come again. storm-washed and thirsting, such surrender to
deliberate annihilation. come away to

vows made in fragrant blood beneath the surge. and return
to the snowlight on the ocean
once more. look, we will learn to see in the dark -   it begins
with defiance and ends

with an untamed sirens call. listen, listen to my weathered
voice on the crescent path

Come.

Home.

Come.

Undone.

Come. Again.

bloodletting

dizzy spells and the heart humming of seashells   your
bones frame me into the ground
whisper. whisper. a song of a city built from water   grey
stories cracked open
once uprooted wild defiance

being covered in blood is a love-language   drowning in
yours is a symphony
so   hand me your cat eyes
so   I may see in your darkness

barely awake   barely asleep

I read your horoscope tonight it is written in your stars
that you will dismantle
this system

and your hand will fit perfectly into mine   trust me - it
comes with being born
at the end of capitalism

my soul is ablaze where your rage flowered in resistance
I carry the curious blossoms on me to the tomb   setting
the stage for the fall
what if   star-crossed meant

setting fire
to the bed
and not the dreams

lost use - overbite

Crown
all is quiet on the vermilion border
she smokes fast, talks faster than the rain
the story of a girl who had her kitten teeth
taken
sutured into a woman
who hasn't lost her bite

Neck
You see, the second line of defence
grows strong from the softest flesh
alchemizes in jagged shorelines
dark red and purple
permanent eruption
to take chunks
out of this wasted glass sky

Root
Extraction to make space
for a mouthful of paper-thin chewing
this crunching night song of bones channels
the words that did not make it
 out alive to dust
the words that at the end of the day
were too hard to swallow

(I hope someone tells you
it takes a lot more muscles to keep your mouth shut
then to open up)

Canal
every dawn adorned with full bloodied lips
I'll lay all these marked bodies
beneath my pillow and call upon

burn it all down, then kiss me

some godmother tonight

Artery, Vein
The girl has a story
a woman maybe more
1 in 3 we have been calculated
measured out to be
fixed in silver, braced and defenceless

Nerve
fed back to the lockjaw of silence
tell me again how to smile
every girl has a story
"you have to stop the bleeding"
it will knock you right out.

love potion

recipe:
- a crude bomb made of a bottle filled with a flammable liquid
  (such as the dirty blood of women)
- fit with a wick (such as a cloth saturated with shame)
- ignite just before the bottle is hurled.

maybe I am on the rag
maybe it is then that I am holy
maybe I will drench it

with all I can give
stuff it in a bottle of gasoline
cast it far   cast it wide

maybe I will watch it all burn
this system only sheds our blood

turn to me now

            watch me bleed

                        myself

                                    free

tfw....you burn the patriarchy to the ground.

Cut the rope, cast the doubts on the pyre. Let's take back these streets tonight.
I see red carnations blossom in the back of your throat tonight.

We come from angry women, the daughters of disturbing the peace. Another voice taken,
no more mournful candles, no more silent vigils.
Tell me how can they sleep peacefully tonight?

Each stolen breath a thousand calls echoing. Make a wish through the tears, every bottle of gasoline
a fallen star in a state of emergency.
We are not afraid to break glass tonight

because we know that this is war. We know to unhinge, to build better than to fix something beyond repair.
We will not keep spare parts tonight.

your hands quivering, I feel a new world waking in your raised fist, just between the heart and the headline, your hair cut and fallen soothsaying all of our fate tonight.

I am the many, I am not alone.
We are bread. We are roses. We are the
"we will burn it all down" - it is not a figure of speech -
we are raising all of hell, all of the earth tonight

to hold up all of the sky. And if they cross beyond the frames of our bones and bodies again, again,
I will hold you, my sister, and tend your wounds in the flare of the bleeding moon tonight.

The old lie: we are the wicked women, the witches and
bitches, the gossip and the fire
with life and freedom in our eyes - the revolutionary blood
of our sisters stays unforgotten tonight.

JIN   JIYAN   AZADI

13 ways of looking at COP27

after Wallace Stevens

I
Among too many suits and ties
The only moving thing
Were the uninvited

II
I am of a thousand tired minds
Like the languid heatwave
In which there are 20,000 corpses

III
Forever chemicals whirl in the autumn rain.
It was a small part of the point of no return.

IV
Love and Rage
Are one.
Love, Rage and your voice bleeding
Are one.

V
I don't know anymore; every Friday
"System change not climate change"
When the flood came, I didn't know
What that meant - my system changed
Internal eternal jetlag

VI
Icicles trickle down, too fast, when was the last
Time you saw one? Do you dream of a blackbird
Or do you see all this barbaric shadow dust?

The Slow Death of an entire generation traced in the ashes
Of
An indecipherable cause.

VII
Old white men, can you imagine
For most of us, there are no golden tickets?
Do you not see how the darkened world is
Crumbling around your fattened-up confessions?
Surely it's not all corporations.
Surely we can buy our way out of this.
Name your price. the moon is littered too.

VIII
I know clever words, mass extinction or biotic crisis,
And lucid, inescapable insights -
But I know, too,
That the money and the fury are involved

IX
When ecocide stays out of Newsnight,
It barely marks the intersecting edge
Of one of many crises.

X
At the sight of people
Protecting the trees with their bare bodies
Bruised forest flowers blossom in green, blue and
Violet. Even the bawds of the law
Might cry silently when no one is watching.

XI
Riding the universe
In a glass house, pockets full of
Anthracite gravel. All the blackbirds are
Dying. A fear pierced the surface

They mistook a stack of burning paper
For change.

XII
The people are moving.
The blood-speckled henchmen should be trembling.

XIII
It was the break of dawn all along.
It was set alight.
And there was going to be a revolt.
The blackbirds sing of upheaval, of transformation,
Of abolition, of crowns burning,
Stretching their limbs.

atropine

oblivion simmers in the rising sun, surrendering the lost
flames to your breath - incinerate the withered memories
with your October eyes

I swallow these belladonna glances - surely, you remember,
I always tend to drown,
shell-shocked and gasping, resurfacing into golden, fawn
coffee

these eyes waking the world, small salvations in the cold
waves, now the small dark death of me
I carve candlelight from the beats
of your crashing heart

sleepless in all the wrong places. Will the day come, will we
stop counting the shadowless nights in beds, eating the
heart? I took your words

to the water at dawn,
cast them across the wisps of fog
seafaring ghosts. They still came back.

Maybe we lost the map. Maybe we are still counting
the losses of yesterday.

> we can still find
>   tomorrow

christmas morning creaks

little treats in your altar bed. the distance is too sore for
silence
I tell you how watering dead gardens in November was
killing

me splitting my sides made you dream of a colder day
flooding and an ice rink tell me again   how you are
not romantic

we both know the butterflies of all these years come from
second
hand anxiety and checking a second horoscope
neurotic charm

wears and tears down faster than fishnets from Primark
          battle worn
we love in ruins   common war zones and under pressure
          cute date idea

you think of fairy lights. I think of broken, splintered
bones. we both stave
off the hounds of hell with honey cakes   a bit of burnt
toast - I am not suicidal- just really kinky

we can be heroes nymphs crazy cat ladies   I thought we
were special   yet nowa-days everyone lives with ghosts
          forever making us jump in the burn of the screen

better cast some more salt I think about how you spill
coffee   it is a festive
spectacle   just let it go   my sweet heart   maybe
we are bad bisexuals

maybe idealism just loves company
we for sure love misery   merry and bright

and dream of worker bees

she knows
the intimacy of strangers
the vanishing nail polish
a compliment to the almond foam

coffee pouring from her hands
knowing the order
eating at everyone's heart

and the pencil in her hair
strawberry blonde
a flushed kind of ginger
an extra shot of espresso
— the Brazilian kind

she knows
dancing between empty cups
and empty people
we are all homeless romantics
I stare at her hands

flat white
leggings and ballerina slippers
signature blend of passionate people pleasers
the sweetest Northern accent
this side of Milan

watch me write these love letters as if
they were poetry, what a performance
a glance lingering

Let's play pretend
to not notice, not recognise
£3.45 for a drop of soul

a dash of feeling alive
all this in-between

she knows
loneliness
caffeine induced tachycardia
my heart jumps off my sleeve
did her hand brush the cup
where I placed my stained lips?

evening prayer

there is beauty
in a revolution
quivering
in the silent places
of the world

I can't hear it anymore
trapped in that night
by the riverside when

I asked you to
lay your fingers
in all my wounds and watch
them bloom

radical   movement

1. Red

the first-night reverie

says it all   marks it

haunting or holiness

mahogany cascades across the pillow

I unearth your heart bone with my bare hands

breathe with me   hold on tight don't stop   *so close*

my old blood initiated your old sheets

I kiss your wrists and drink deep

all that falling

the floorboards creaked under the tension

of what could be

of what we left behind

a soft skylight

in this home wreck

I wondered what keeps up the roof

burn it all down, then kiss me

a single beam of dark wood

I like to hold onto things   *it makes me feel better*

these cold shades of grey

we will paint them black

raking the moon for the scent of spring

the push and the pull

there are no doors here   only frames

do you want to come

inside?

2. Wood

sharing your bed in winter

still holds the warmth of

a summer in shallow   water

you   feverish burning in the dark

your willow eyes   set me free

and when I feel your currents around me at nightfall

I always return with you   to the forest

take roots here   and extend them

        outwards

intertwine in the living groves   something so

good after the rain

to withstand the flood

caught in nightmares

we could never escape the dream

burn it all down, then kiss me

(I)ignite

A bucket-wheel excavator consumes an average of 200,000 kW a day - electricity enough for a small town with 17,000 inhabitants.

I.
I walked slowly towards
the edge of the world
eyes front, a single black flag
courageously torn
I hold tight to

all these abandoned cities
all these forests fallen and fled
all the rivers poisoned and thin
inside of me

it is hard to keep the score of everything lost
in this economy
it is hard to conserve some energy
for the crises
This is where home lies.

except it doesn't

not even a ghost
town to bear
witness to skeleton houses

haunted with riches
excavated like
the bones of
ancient creatures

why can't we stop visiting these graves?
the metallic growl carried on the wind

dust to dust.
we live and die with the ashes
flowing on every breath

talk me off the ledge but
I won't ever get myself to wipe off
the soot on my boots
I want to walk past the picket fences
with proof of this wound
always with me
for all to see

look, this is where it hurts.

II.
how dare we just stand here
at the break-off edge of the sleeping soil
with nothing but stolen dreams
and empty promises
when the house has already burnt down?

what do we want?
what did we want
when we were given it all?
what do we want?
the prayer is left unfinished.

an antidote
to the generational curse of
wake work die
repeat

lies
in each other's arms
in tearing down the walls
in building the barricade higher

burn it all down, then kiss me

than the profit margin

let me feel the songs of the dying earth
in the palm of your hand
in each beat of every heartbreaking
where the ground has been
made unholy

this is where we all bleed
this is where it hurts
this is where it ends

this is where they bury us
this is where we cover them
in the flowers of disobedience
this is where resistance blossoms
a fireweed set ablaze

it is never civil. it's
new blood and no regrets
hope is untameable and wild
it feeds on the rotting heart
of the ever-starving beast

it is burning.
it is dreaming.
it is. waking up.

keep it in the ground
keep it in the ground
keep it in the ground
keep it in the ground
keep it in the ground
keep it in the ground
keep it in the ground
keep it in the ground
keep it in the ground
keep it in the ground
keep it in the ground
keep it in the ground
keep it in the ground
keep it in the ground
keep it in the ground
keep it in the ground
keep it in the ground
keep it in the ground
keep it in the ground
keep it in the ground
keep it in the ground
keep it in the ground
keep it in the ground
keep it in the ground
keep it in the ground
keep it in the ground
keep it in the ground
keep it in the ground
keep it in the ground
keep it in the ground
keep it in the ground
keep it in the ground

keep it in
keep it in

It is treason to stop dreaming.

burn it all down, then kiss me

III.
this is where it hurts
on the edge
again, again
sentenced to death
on the smothering wound
always running, digging
us deeper into a catastrophe
nothing makes you feel as alive
as seeing violent times
as violently holding hands

whisper we must love another or we die
keep your head up
stare down the police line
we wear armour too
wrapped around each other
heart-to-heart, sleeve to sleeve
answer the call
another world is possible

deconstruct.
reassemble.
gather each other
up.

remember, eyes front
I'll face you when we splinter.
crash into me and I will hold
its only fire
raining from all the lovers
burning
with you
in this storm

and yes it stings

and yes it bruises, blossoms
teal, dark deep blue
throbs for decades
all these colours
all this glistening

can't be evicted from our bones
the earth here knows our tale
and maybe we saw something die
but whatever trembles,
grows in the dark, within you

is safe with me
is safe with you
the frontier isn't them or us
we are aligned on the last breaths
drawn from the ancient dirt and dust

IV.
red
the trickle beneath
the eye
red
the flags
we raise
call off the search
we are here
we survived saved
even ourselves

knowing now
there are no shortcuts
to dreams come true
if you cry - wail
if you laugh - roar
if you are filled with love and rage

burn it all down, then kiss me

bring it all down
unto us
for the great unlearning
arranging all the new stars into constellations
that spell
change

yes, if you start a fire
yes, you will burn
yes, you will light up the world
strike now

V.
in this game of numbers
we shall know revolution
and stand like trees
in the hymnal winter mud
naked, rooted, mined
this soil is a rich song of reckoning

we won more than we lost

take my raw skin
and let me bleed next to you
on the fields
crying for battle
but seeding hope
my eyes flooded
you wash the defeat away
open them softly to the light
of another world dawning

today there is almost nothing
today there is almost everything

bed and roses

Idk…
I am under a spell
send for demon daddy
or the exorcist
maybe some coffee
and vanilla ice cream
and a cigarette
call for change
while you're at it

will we just lay here?

when a storm spills onto the street
the hand throwing a rock
is holding
a first kiss
between what is
and what could be

injured parties born from
the fire in your eyes
it lights up this dying world

cover me in ashes, darling.

forfeit

I lay down in a bed
of summer's end
of reeds and sand
of a thousand deaths
the last fireflies
grieving for the river

elevated on a free surface
I will sink
drown dreaming
soundly ablaze
dancing on your lips
a confession

   it is not a coffin
   it is a renaissance of the moon
   and loneliness burning at dusk

I would unfurl your hands
like withered leaves
delicate and hardened
dried with the heat crushing
at the very end of the world

are you afraid?

land softly in the fern and moss
of my wishing bones

are you alive?

phrasing my darling
like a question
it leaves this phantom wound

starcrossed on my throat
so oblivious
so obliterated
by my silence

does a door stay open
or does it remain shut
if you tear off the handle?

when the sun sets
and the path is untaken

if only this fleeting light
could show you
how I fell

on my bloodied knees
to drink
your waters

burn it all down, then kiss me

oaktown

and when they ripped open
the heart of the earth

this heart of
our ancient home

the forests within us
began to grow

storms broke from
our hoarse throats

and amidst the
Dark Walls
closing in

we found each other's eyes —
our roots digging deep

we would not fall

broken bones

built a home

bleed me out gently

don't open your eyes yet
the want is ravaged and set alight
I will call your pain to me
name your beasts to do my bidding

call me back

to worship with wanton knees and eyes
nail my collarbones to the bedroom door
and drink from my bruised lips
a dream like this demands a hungered sacrifice

call me back

to your kingdom on this starless night
the rain so reckless in the shadows
let me dream of your trembling spine
and pry open your butterfly ribs

call me back

to plant moonflowers in your blood
they only bloom carefree in the dark
let me honour you with what remains
beyond skin and crushed days

call me back

to your bed, your voice drowns
out the world. Was it even real?
I just want to feel you - here and here.
all I touch is glass

all hallowed

to be read in case of emergency

we crossed this ocean /I lost the ground / the moon
drew me/in /my crimson tides /beckoning your hands
in red /on the mirroring surface / the light of early dawn

come
falling
apart

celestial bodies of water / on the fine shoreline before
sleep
betroth my hands / to your breath/your elfin throat
vowing /gasping / on half of the dead stars
to be strange / to be beautiful / to be wild / to be

open water

crashing on broken shells / blessed October sand
a litany / a siren song / an unchanging state of affairs
I am not going to hurt you /cannot resist the call of
continued disturbance and fractures on the wind

a tear bled / into black ink stains/blossoms / into a word
echoes into a constant dream yet untold /let's send a
postcard

from
where
we
fell

some things are better on paper /some things are better
signed and sealed / in blood

mountain ash

tell me
tell me of the August nights
sitting up in your bed
waiting for the dawn

our city sunken in sweltering sleep
while I hold your scarred hand
how we dance a little drunkenly
on the edge of the void
and the dreamscape

the rope work is elaborate
but cuts the skin
falling
stars burn up
when returned to the unholy ground

let's paint their names on our walls
and follow the flames

pour dark sunflower resin on
the moonlight cast from my eyes
haunt me for a while longer
I will not capture your light

there's an amber trail
in the quivering of your words
a magnitude for
the earth opening beneath me

and what if I fall?
what if we jump?

understory

meet me in the woods
where we died
where we still hang
from cobwebs listening to
summer weeping with gale songs
for the legend of two ill-timed lovers
forever rooted on the crossroads

I'll take you to the clearing
and run some old ghosts up your spine
they all think they are holy, lovelorn
— and we respect the dead here

blink twice and you will miss it
I engrave this night upon your skin
with incandescent thorns and
the breath of an ancient goddess
scratching out the past

and if I cut you too deep
grant me to take out the stitches
I'll let you hold onto the threads
and bind you in your wishes

we will just pretend they are mine

welcome the soul back to the
quiet, the warm cadence
of a silence that follows the thunder
a voice but no tongue to speak
a deathly stir in the leaves is not a lullaby

please listen, do you hear what I am saying
when I tell you it is hunting season

for demons but don't worry,
love, I'll bring a toolbox to the forest
we'll use the spare parts
of what is beyond repair

reassemble for a new day
water those burnt-out thickets
various stages of moonlit decomposition
above the soil
watch them feed
watch them blossom
in the dark

burn it all down, then kiss me

the warm blood crashes

the warm blood crashes
don't turn on the light
move across the dark

moonlike from surrender to resurrection
drink red wine from raspberry jam glasses
and fall for the elm fires

we can burn everything down
rise from the ashes
forget to remember
we were once here

Kate MacAlister

mundane mourning

dare to see the scrying mirror
in the obsidian half-light
we will sleep when we are dead

until then we will break
each other out of every prison

in the candlelight, I hide all the broken glass
sing raw urgent hymns
to your scars

watch what is written on the walls
the flickering words fading in the distance
planted on our past

when a home has crumpled and taken apart
before the end of the tenancy

come sit in the wilderness with me
watch the transactional passing of theorems

time has bid me goodbye
floated away on the tremors of your voice

at least once
it'll be perfect

to be held
not to be handled

remember when you painted me red?

let me help you
draw out this poison
from every chamber
of your heart

but know that
my mouth
is full of lies
as we tumble through

all the throes
and the thresholds
the shattering glass
the white shirts

the silenced weight of the world
on our chests
looking back only once more
my eyes grasp for hers

ancient embers of pyromantic rebellion
sweeping through their cities
built on sand
the only lesson learnt

we don't live
by their
rules anymore

guerrilla girl art

You read this book
Countless beautiful absurdities
A story cabinet filled to the brim
With poison and wine
Something strange to behold like
Bone fires
Or the silence of men

"He painted flowers on her starving body,
Blue orchids and Valerian in the dying night"

So I pick up my pen to
trace your
Tiger stripes
And Leylines
Back home
By the light
Of Stars
Blossoming
Beneath your eyes

and these are the flowers of the partisan

we stopped living in houses
already torn down
there is no treasure
at the end
of the rubble

we garden in the moonlight
the dark is medicine
for our sisters
carnations planted
for those voices lost

the soil is rich with a story
of love unbound
a story within stories

within you
within me

a myth waiting to be assembled
birthed in the light of
dying stars

Kate MacAlister

burn it all down then kiss me

I map you out   beneath the falling stars
we know our way   we didn't get lost at all
on the overgrown riverbank,   the candles burn all night
I would let you   take me   down

maybe we can find your places here at the bottom of it all
we can turn each stone   skip the surface watch each
other
dance in the ripples   of this alluvial mirror

                              it was not the end.

maybe we could move   to the city of lights   or the
edge of the forest
the end of the world   so bewildered in your depths
          ask me again

how I would liberate you on the left side of my bed
how you would free me entangled in your pain

crushed and suffocated against the bedroom wall
I'll bring you coffee when you breathe again

I am not catching feelings I am catching fire

sometimes we spell

                    love   revolt

love language

lay down with me
the floor beneath my walls
is sticky with betrayal

I will shatter
every bottle,
every glass
in this cupboard
the ceiling
make the whole house tremble

walk in the shards
with bare feet to
bleed myself free

but tonight
hold me in your gentle hands

speak to me of love
speak to me of change
tell me it is on its way

speak to me of the way your grandma used to dance
speak to me of an alleycat greeting you on your way home
speak to me of how you had to fall to conquer the
mountain or
speak to me of that one time when you lay in the lake
and whispered to the moon, watching the falling stars

speak to me of the wilderness inside of you
the darkness always trembling towards the light
speak to me of our sisters holding hands
walking through the ashes of what was

speak to me of love
speak to me of change
speak to me of turning it all around
while the world
shakes and burns
in our quivering hands
barely touching
speak to me,
Love.

& rage

let's believe we are   braver than the storm
rushed and normalised
for survival   bargaining for freedom left with zero hours
          minimum wage
we will cry in the dark   break out   a tune
carry it gracefully
into that rotting heart

for the resistance is everywhere

knowing exactly
what
is burning
at   the
stake

knowing exactly
there are words
that light up all of
these ruins

knowing exactly
others set the world on fire
burn cities to the ground

let's say   let's believe for a second   that it is radical
to draw poison from the root with bared teeth
let's really believe we were comfortable
inside   the cage
even when the floor creaks and snaps
an ever-crunching sound
the mortar of blood and bone   of every stranger
every sister   yours and mine

let's say it is time to be up in arms
let's believe no one is left behind
when we tear it all down
brick by brick   washing it away
the coal and the oil
the fear
of missing
out

left with zero hours left with nothing
but love and rage
we were always going to be

too late
too late
how romantic

the only date
in permanent crisis

the only moment
that counts is
now

awakening   still /again

christmas morning constellations traced on your skin /
undressed / spilt / beneath the quivering lashes and
breathless light /enfolded below the midwinter dawn/ so
stolen between

the call of the day and the coffee /(do you want to go and
see the worst of me?) /clothes on the creaking floor / a
tangible whisper in the curtains / the red farewell /stars
sighing in your image

and the resurrection of today/ sheltered twilight /can't hide
the embers mined in / the dead of night / still on my lips /
I am still starving /my heart half eaten / still obsessed/
with what remains

of the distant bedrock / the thunderwounds
of yesterday / (do I not burn when I bleed?)
I hold your hand/ through these hurting dreams to support
their weight
still /again

we summoned and witnessed / an unspeakable trinity
come / here / tonight /

Despair
Desire
& the small Death

(prayer is whatever you say on your knees) and if you can't
forgive what lurks below the skin
remember / I am fire-tongued and anointed by your touch
/deciphering the holy infliction
of having been wild and perfect for a moment / (thirst to
thirst) / surrender now

(your fingers in my hair / my mouth / covered in my
blood) / hold me / in this space

we are rebuilding the universe / my words are the bare
bones
painted with the colours
you have
shown me
/ l o v e /

this is how we retaliate / desecrate the decaying temple
with solemn lunar devotions
feral laments / spellbound in the marked sheets/
the unmade bed

burn it all down, then kiss me

hypnagogia

sleep and remember   the last kiss good night

(this is the last time)

up against these walls   of mine
in the gallery of trembling promises

how we lay in the dark
         observing
all the crushed petals of
love-me-nots   withered and died
here we were once
excavated works of art   signed off by the pain
of having lived   limited edition
conserved and flattened beneath safety glass

how we lay next to the skeleton of this haunting
                 shrouded

(it's still breathing)

and we still stare   in wonder
eyelash to eyelash
falling   fallen

it is almost too late for this reverie
to walk in the hungered night air
when every beat   of heart upon heart
is an oath
to wake the witch at dawn
foreseeing broken   resurrection

how we lay beneath
the fractured moonlight
casting handfuls of stars   into the void

Kate MacAlister

a wishing well

kiss me harder   than I remember

your story blood in my mouth
is good enough
in this moment

sleep and remember   this is the last time

burn it all down, then kiss me

take care of each other

rain is coming, arrive in my hand
lock eyes

give me a new reason to tremble
to keep moving

I'll name the shadow following you
if the door is broken up and

wide, call me and I will fuel
your fires

come to my heart not for
repair but a blessing
for what is broken

I'll catch your tears come dawn
watering what goes out
of line

let me teach you the spell of
compassion, fury, experience - patience

I'll catch you every time
I can - not every time you
fall

tear down the picket fence
never cross the picket line
keep a light on whether the nights are
too long or too short
we are unstoppable
with the intention
of declaring class war

Kate MacAlister

to be dangerous together

throat to the sky, open.
link arms

we are the long shadows of better days
cast upon the wasted earth

we might be dead
tomorrow - today we breathe, grow in the dark

dance in the sea of infinite possibility
of having nothing - of having to give
everything

let my words, these songs in the streets
tell you what democracy looks like

be a wild river to float your defiance
back home to love

cantations are born in the stillness
and made by the embers of defiance

caught in the currents stirring unrest among the people

we won't settle for what we can get
we lay trails with the crumbs and swallow stars

it's a team effort
to fuck the system, a practice of worship

call and response, bring in all the voices
your scream initiating us to bear witness
to the sacred ceremony of care
another world is possible

burn it all down, then kiss me

    with the intention
    of declaring it a love language

References

The following references are sources of inspiration, research, or allusion to the poems in this collection.

r i t u a l

was inspired by Diane di Prima's "Loba Part 1"

summoning

The Fates – or Moirai – are a group of three weaving goddesses who assign individual destinies to mortals at birth. Their names are Clotho (the Spinner), Lachesis (the Alloter) and Atropos (the Unturnable).

They are the fatherless daughters of Nyx, the Night and their decisions could not be changed by even the most powerful gods.

may queen

This poem was written during my time working as a nurse in the NICU during the first lockdown in 2020.
This poem holds the experience of my first brush with death.

I never knew such fear, humility, exhaustion and urgency. Yet it taught me that next to fear, death and loss there will always be more love and kindness. And that there is no greater gift and honour than being able to help even if it is just to ease the loneliness that this virus and this society has brought upon us.

That being said - medical staff and nurses deserve fair wages and working conditions that do not push them out of the profession.

lost use - overbite

The subtitles follow the anatomical/histological structure of teeth.

atropine

Atropine occurs naturally in various parts of plants such as the deadly nightshade. It is used in medicine to dilate pupils and increase the heart rate.

tfw....you burn the patriarchy to the ground.

"Jin, Jiyan, Azadî" is the basis, the guiding principle and the slogan of the Kurdish freedom movement. Jin and Jiyan, meaning woman and life, originate from the same word root in Kurdish and symbolize the close connection between the meaning of woman and life. Azadî means freedom. In the Kurdish freedom movement, it is said that a society can only be as free as the women in this society are. It places women's freedom at the centre of its struggle for a liberated life without oppression.

For decades, the Kurdish freedom movement has been criminalized and persecuted for this fight, and its members have been imprisoned and murdered.

(l)ignite

Luetzerath is a village near Cologne, in the Rhineland lignite mining area, Europe's largest source of carbon emissions. Lignite coal, the most climate-damaging energy source, is mined and burnt here by the cooperation RWE. For 2.5 years, people have been occupying the village of Luetzerath to block the expansion of the Garzweiler II mine and to fight against the worldwide destruction of our climate.

bed & roses

References to "Choreomania" by Florence & the Machine

oaktown

In September 2018, Hambach Forest was about to be deforested. It is a remnant of 2 km² of the originally 40 km² large Bürgewald, between Cologne and Aachen, which has been cleared since 1978 for the Hambach opencast mine.

The tree house colony there and the protests in the Hambach Forest are symbols of resistance to lignite mining, coal-fired power generation and the associated climate pollution. Since 2012, the remaining part of the forest has been occupied by activists several times.

Oaktown was a protest camp in the struggle to save the forest.

Previously Published Works

'May Queen' was first published in HerWords, Black Mountain Press 2021

'melusine', 'burn it all down and kiss me' was first published in Tahmina, Free Verse Revolution 2022

'and these are the flowers of the partisan' was first published in Stimmen der Rebellion/Dengê Berxwedane/Voices of Rebellion Issue 1 2022

'Canticle', 'Bed & Roses', 'Guerrilla Girl Art' and 'forfeit' were first published in the quarterly anthologies of Querencia Press 2022

'Blood Letting', 'understory' were first published in Gypsophila - the white- Volume 2 Issue 3 2022

(L)ignite was first published in aah! Magazine Manchester Metropolitan University Press 2023

'awakening still/again', 'all hallowed' & 'bleed me out gently' were first published in South Broadway Ghost Society 2023

'tfw…you burn the patriarchy to the ground' was first published in Stimmen der Rebellion/Dengê Berxwedane/Voices of Rebellion Issue 2 2023

About the Poet

"When we share our stories, we realize that we are not alone with it. We begin to see the system that is behind violence, injustice and exploitation. Telling our story is the connecting moment to take action and to initiate change."

Kate MacAlister (she/her) is an author, feminist socialist activist and founder of the multilingual community arts and literature project Stimmen der Rebellion/Dengê Berxwedane/Voices of Rebellion. She has studied Creative Writing at the Manchester Writing School under the tutelage of Carol Ann Duffy.

Her works have been published in journals and anthologies all over the world and featured in multi-disciplinary performance art projects. Kate's debut chapbook "songs of the blood" is filled with poetry that speaks of human connection and the dreams of revolution. Coffee, her cat Bella and, naturally, her activist friends are particularly important for her creative process. Find Kate on Instagram at @kissed.by_fire.

Other books by this Poet

songs of the blood, Querencia Press 2022

About the Publisher

Sunday Mornings at the River is a poetry publisher that is dedicated to elevating and amplifying the voices of poets who are often marginalized or overlooked by the traditional publishing world.

At Sunday Mornings at the River, we are committed to creating a thriving literary community that is based on healthy and inclusive collaborations. We believe that everyone has the right to be heard, and we strive to provide a platform for poets to share their work with a wider audience.

Our focus is on publishing poetry that is thought-provoking, challenging, and speaks to the unnamable aspects of the human experience. We believe that poets have the power to name the frauds, take sides, start arguments, and shape the world, and we are always on the lookout for new voices that are pushing the boundaries of traditional poetry.

As an independent publisher, we are dedicated to promoting equality and inclusivity in all of our endeavours. Whether we are working with established authors or helping emerging poets to get their work out into the world, we are committed to creating a welcoming and supportive environment for poets of all backgrounds and experiences.

Acknowledgements

I am immensely grateful to all feminist and climate activists, who have been at the forefront of the struggles against the violence perpetrated by capitalist exploitation. Your relentless efforts in the fight for social justice, and environmental sustainability are the reason for me to keep telling the stories of love and resistance.

To all my comrades and friends, who have despaired, hoped, protested, and fought alongside me, thank you for your unwavering support, tender hearts and solidarity.

To the witches and feminist sweethearts. Your unapologetic fierceness, wisdom, and organising have changed me forever and let my rebellion blossom into words. Your collective power and unrelenting spirit have set me on fire. Together, we will burn down the patriarchy — and build a world free of poverty, oppression and violence.

To Carlotta, my revolutionary flame. Your passion, dedication, and resilience have been the deep, red-heart blood of my poetry and have given me so much courage to keep on fighting for a different world. For women, life and freedom.

To Laura, Lina, Lisa and Fatma. We have stood side by side, lifting each other up for all these years, and I am forever grateful for your unwavering friendship and the revolutionary love we offer up to each other again and again.

To Moritz, for showing me how to find the starlight on the dark ocean and how to retrieve dreams from rock bottom - even if you lost the map.

A very special thanks to my beloved and admired Susan Parenti - who shared her wisdom, poetry and rebellious spirit with me. For telling me "you are a writer if you call yourself just that".

A very special thanks also goes to my kindred soul Paul Kaiser for all the vulnerable cups of coffee and sharing of poems to change the world - in small-town America.

To the countless women and queer people who have shared their stories, struggles, and triumphs with me, thank you for your bravery and vulnerability. You have taught me the true meaning of hope.

To the Manchester Writing School and all the brilliant writers I was granted to encounter here: thank you for showing me the path leading to a life of poetry.

And thank you to Becks, the Boss Lady of Sunday Mornings at the River for believing in poetry as direct action and taking a chance on my writing.

Also : Lützi bleibt.

Scan me
for more books
by Sunday Mornings
at the River

w: sundaymorningsattheriver.com
e: hello@sundaymorningsattheriver.com
ig: @sundaymorningsattheriver
t: @smatrpress

Printed in Poland
by Amazon Fulfillment
Poland Sp. z o.o., Wrocław

30727553R00050